STRETCHIN

The Race toward Diversity
Equity and Inclusion in America

M000087707

STRETCHING: The Race toward Diversity, Equity, and Inclusion in America

Published by:
Savvy Dimension Publishing
www.chauncia.com

Book Creation and Design
DHBonner Virtual Solutions, LLC
www.dhbonner.net

ISBN for Hardcover: 978-1-7361593-0-9
ISBN for Paperback: 978-1-7361593-1-6
ISBN for eBook: 978-1-7361593-2-3

Printed in the United States of America

This book is dedicated to Mom and Dad.

Table of Contents

With Special Thanks

This book is about overcoming the disasters of life to ascend to a plateau where dreams become reality.

I am eternally grateful to my God for comforting me in the most extraordinary ways during my darkest of days. Your gentleness and loving kindness were manna to my soul. You, Lord, continue to carefully order my steps toward a life filled with an abundance of love and acceptance.

To those who have supported me in speaking my truth and encouraged me to use my voice for a greater purpose, I thank you.

To the *Institute for Diversity and Inclusion in Emergency Management* family, thank you. Curtis Brown, Ellis Stanley, Sr., Antoine Richards, and so many more, your friendship and passion for disaster justice keeps my inner flame lit.

Finally, I would like to acknowledge with tremendous love and gratitude my family: my parents, Mary and Elijah; my sisters, Che'Rese and Courtney; my brothers-in-law, Matthew Sr. and Tony; my son, Michael Elijah, and so many more. Your unconditional love and support is a blessing.

"To control a people, you must first control what they think about themselves and how they regard their history and culture."
-Dr. John Henrik Clarke

INTRODUCTION:
The Best Kept Secret

S tretching: *The Race Toward Diversity, Equity, and Inclusion in America* is a call to action for those who have experienced or witnessed the injustice of discrimination and now seek a deeper understanding of the value of diversity, equity, and inclusion.

I'm going to be transparent with you — right from the beginning. I didn't realize I'd be writing a book at this time. Let's be real. In a workspace that lacks a reflection of those who look like me, I am a Black woman who has invested two decades of my career into an industry that doesn't promote people like me — why wouldn't I write about it?

However, the more I thought about it, the more I realized that my life's story is truly a testament to the value of diversity, equity, and inclusion. Though painful to think about, much less write about, I know that my story needs to be told and my perspective shared. As a Black woman, my perspective is rarely expressed, heard, and received without judgment. I believe the viewpoint of Black women operating in male-dominated fields hasn't been acknowledged and understood, which has precluded our ability to have our voices heard and to be who we truly are, our whole selves when the majority at the table don't understand that our seat at that same table brings so much more than just the brown skin we're in.

Often, there is an attempt to mute or diminish a Black woman's experiences, or worse yet, seek to explain our experiences from another person's perspective. Among several attributes, there is one thing in particular that I love and admire about Black women . . . that is their courage in times of battle. We employ the innate strength of our lived experiences to stretch our capacity to move beyond striving to thriving, dependent to interdependent, and vulnerable to resilient like no one else!

And so, while I have had humiliatingly heartbreaking moments throughout my career, I embrace the discomfort of sharing my story so that I might personalize the shared experiences of many others who are like me, those who have never found acceptance within the workplace because you are who you are. This book is written from a place that identifies with those who have told themselves not to cry while being talked down to in a meeting; the single moms and dads wondering if they should complain about discrimination or harassment, knowing they have little ones at home and mouths to feed, and for all those who try as you might, still don't "belong."

I have been an Emergency Manager for years and tend to look at life in the stages of disaster: Preparedness, response, mitigation, recovery, and ultimately, resilience. In many ways, life is a cycle of disaster, and we are all emergency managers that go from one crisis to the next, hoping to avoid loss or negative impacts, so we can recover and return to normal. I have worked with all sorts of people, from the White House to the crack house, and I can honestly say, no one is exempt from the disasters of life.

Major calamities like job loss, the death of a loved one, sickness, divorce, etc., happen to everyone at some point, whether you are rich or poor. Even those temporary crises like speeding tickets, fender benders, and lost keys will prick your finger at some point. It's inevitable: Disasters will come, and they can, unfortunately, destabilize life and compound hardship. However, with a bit of savvy, they can become unexpected opportunities for growth and change.

THE BEST KEPT SECRET

Now, I love to watch great orators speak, and often, I will review their speeches in great depth. A favorite of mine is from the now-deceased pastor, Dr. Myles Monroe, who once preached a sermon about the best-kept secret, and it spoke to me in many ways. His sermon described the abundance of treasure that resides in every cemetery. Like me, you might assume the treasure is found in the casket in the form of valuable jewelry or possibly the gold teeth grave robbers used to steal.

But no, the treasure is not the jewelry and tangible items the dead might be buried with; it is the untapped dreams and potential that went with them when they died. In Pastor

Monroe's estimation, the untapped power of potential is the real treasure that cannot be seen or recovered.

As I listened to his sermon, I determined that there was another dormant treasure; yet this one hides in plain sight, not in a cemetery. This secret gem is complex and contemplative, but like Beyonce, it requires commitment. It is a valuable treasure and has a tremendous impact when employed, yet still, it dwells in the world of the unknown and underappreciated. And even though it has the power to generate innovation, make space for belonging, and lead to organizational transformation, it is perceived as an existential threat.

So, you ask, what is this thing, this concept that I am speaking of? And why does it create fear and get maligned as an evil to be avoided? These are great questions. No worries, I will tell you. The best-kept secret around is the power of DEI:

Diversity, Equity, and *Inclusion.*

DEI has the power to change the world, and yet, many have no concept of its strength. Though it has been around for quite a while, the immense strength of DEI remains untapped for various reasons. Some folks are just not interested in the additional work of applying concepts that can be challenging to operationalize and that may not directly benefit them. Let's be honest . . . we know that many view DEI as a threat that could end in personal displacement, so they vigorously refute and negate its unused potential. Others see its immediate rewards as a performative, check the box opportunity, and never tap into an embedded, sustainable effort that allows DEI's maximum power to be unveiled.

Despite the intentional and unintentional attempts to minimize the power of DEI, many organizations have discovered its remarkable benefits and now have access to enormous potential to become productive powerhouses of thought and leadership equipped to meet the needs of the diverse groups in our nation.

I have always had a very active imagination and frequently wonder what a world without discrimination and bias would look like. The vision is massive and requires many systemic changes; I find myself getting overwhelmed and must make an effort to deconstruct them one system at a time. I suppose the feeling of overwhelm is what some leaders experience when considering the commitment of time, funding, and effort to DEI within their organization. However, without tapping into the absolute power of diversity, equity, and inclusion, millions of corporations, governments, non-profits, families, and individuals will miss the mark, and their highest potential, including profits, will never be realized.

So, the best-kept secret is diversity, equity, and inclusion; therefore, organizations that prioritize diversity, equity, and inclusion are making a clear decision to commit to tapping into a superpower that has lain dormant. We must get to the point where we view diversity, equity, and inclusion as a superpower, not a burden or additional requirement. Superpowers are not tolerated; they are celebrated. And who doesn't love the Black Panther, Superman, and Wonder Woman?

Well, I am aware that some of you may have initially picked up this book, saw the words diversity, equity, and inclusion in the subtitle, and decided not to read it based on a simplistic understanding of what the words mean. However, this book is not about merely adding more diverse people to an office photo. Instead, in 'Stretching: The Race Toward Diversity, Equity, and Inclusion,' I will introduce you to the value of DEI; we must divest ourselves of biased, limiting constraints and instead stretch far and wide to tap into DEI's untapped potential. I will unpack my own experiences with racism, gender bias, job loss, and resilience as I, myself, stretch towards a more in-depth, poignant knowledge of DEI and its true potential. And as we travel the pages of 'Stretching' together, I will ask you to honestly reflect upon your life and your interpretation of DEI in America — right now and in the future.

As you read through the chapters that follow, be mindful of your own experience and open to considering how you can begin to embody the qualities and characteristics of diversity, equity, and inclusion within your chosen profession, workplace, industry, or community. Be ready to expand your thinking. Allow yourself to be stretched!

PART ONE:
PREPAREDNESS
Childhood Perspectives and Influences

> "Don't allow them to create a space in your mind
> where you begin to doubt your own value."
> -Terry McMillan

Elijah, my paternal grandfather, was murdered — beaten to death by law enforcement in Jackson, Mississippi, in the 60s — long before I was born. He was a talented carpenter, and as a relatively young man, he had become an alcoholic, which speaks to the psychology of that time, considering that men didn't have a way to cope with everything that was happening, other than to drink, chase women, or engage in activities that weren't necessarily beneficial for the family. So, unfortunately, early death was the legacy of many Black men.

Ironically, it still is.

I can remember Ma'dear telling us about how she knew he was dead before anyone told her because he visited her immediately following. When she saw him, she asked, "Eli, what you doing?" And he walked across the bedroom, through the wall, and then left. . . leaving her to raise nine kids alone.

PREPARED FOR ADVERSITY

Although I was born in St. Petersburg, Florida, in the mid-70s, miles and years apart from that seemingly singular event, the impact of it reverberated throughout time and distance to continually affect the life I would be birthed into. Just hearing my dad talk about the poverty he was raised in, being picked on for being poor and very light-skinned because my grandfather had been half German and my grandmother half Native-American (braids and all), and for generally not having enough of whatever it is, still brings tears to my eyes today. He has always been adamant that we should never pick on someone, especially for things they cannot change.

Then, a short drive from Jackson, on the way to Vicksburg, we have my maternal grandfather in Utica, Grandpa Willie. He was a skilled shoe repairman, handsome and congenial . . . and the town alcoholic (He wasn't the town alcoholic, he was just one of many). He just wasn't good with the coping mechanisms needed to handle the day-to-day trauma that Black folk back then (and now) had to contend with. Even when my two sisters and I would visit during the summers, we would "walk uptown" to go to the country grocery store to get candy, we encountered the owner, Terry Clan — a big, white man who towered over us at about six feet and four inches tall, complete with a bulbous nose and huge belly — who would look over at us and ask, "Whose chillin' are y'all? Who's your kinfolk?" A question that was intended to validate our presence and ownership and resembled having to show a "slave pass" — our papers to move outside the plantation.

Therefore, although terrified, we had to answer and identify our family connection because they weren't just going to let Black kids walk around freely in the store. "Our grandfather is Willie Beecham, sir." After a pause, he replied in his southern drawl, "Y'all Willie Bingham kids? You tell your granddaddy to come back here and pay his bill. Now, go on and get what you want, but he better pay his bill by Friday."

Additionally, other white folks had no issue speaking down to us, telling us to get out of their way while expecting us to respond immediately *and politely* to whatever their request, question, or demand. We always said ma'am and sir to anyone older than us, but most especially to white folk. After all, my mother had taught us all about poor Emmitt Till, so we knew that we needed to be overly respectful to whites to get home safely.

Now, my grandfather's dad, my maternal great-grandfather, was Boss Bingham, who was believed to be a quadroon or mulatto man, according to the census paperwork. Imagine that, right? In such a segregated place during the day, apparently is not so at night, as many Black folks in the U.S. have white, Anglo ancestry. However, in those days and to some extent even now, having that one drop of Black blood means that you are Black in America, and unless you are white representing, you will be treated as a Black person. That is why, at a young age, we quickly learn the dynamics of race; we realize as a young person of color, the white male is the default setting, and white men are in charge.

Willie's wife, Sandra Lee, my maternal grandmother, supposedly came from the Geechee tribe of the Carolinas. That side of the family was in the back-breaking business of sharecropping, a vicious form of indentured servitude that epitomizes structural inequities with generational impacts. From what I've been told, her sister, my great-aunt, would make money selling the other family kids into sharecropping; each time, a family member had to find the kids and get them back.

Later, when my grandfather lost the shoe repair shop, they lived on a chicken farm, raising chickens, in a town so poor, it used to have only one stoplight, and we could easily walk uptown or downtown. And, like my father, my mom talks about how they got picked on for being extremely poor as well, and how some would wear potato sacks to school because they didn't have clothes.

She always stressed the importance of being a friend to those who had no friends or didn't fit in well. I imagine she understood the exclusion and loneliness brought on by poverty. Less talked about is the lifelong feeling of shame and insecurity that poverty provokes, and coupled with the intense Mississippi racism, it is a wonder she made it out with her head on right.

We had a lot of family throughout Mississippi, so on those summer trips, Mom would put the three of us on a bus, tell the bus driver, "Watch out for my girls," and we would ride Trailways or Greyhound up to Mississippi by ourselves, with our pork chop sandwiches or greasy fried chicken on white bread in aluminum foil. I miss those days; however, I wouldn't dream of doing that now with my kid for safety reasons. But times were different then . . . and once we arrived in Jackson, our aunt met us as we got off the bus and took us back to her house. After a while, she drove us on the long drive over to our maternal Grandma's house in Utica, where we got to see all of our cousins and stayed for the remainder of the summer.

Being in that environment helped me understand the value of family and the intricate nature of community; the stories shared with me and the experiences I had there are a significant part of the foundation that makes up my upbringing because I thought it was normal.

It *was* normal.

"In every conceivable manner, the family is link to our past, bridge to our future."

-Alex Haley

LIVING WHILE BLACK

Still, as that little girl growing up and traveling back and forth between Florida and Mississippi, initially, I didn't know that I was *Black*. I didn't know that I was all these things that society considered bad, unacceptable, or less than. I didn't know that my skin color had a stigma attached to it. Unfortunately, for most of us, there is a defining moment when you become cognizant that you are perceived differently and need to accommodate other people's perspectives. So, there is an indoctrination that occurs, a bias that we have to live beyond, to move past, or to function around; at least, until we become mature enough not to care what other people think. Admittedly, it took me a while to get to that place of understanding.

For many Black people, we don't get to be just kids playing in the park. Beyond the age of six, we aren't regarded as innocent children. Black boys and girls are viewed as older than their peers — our girls are oversexualized, and our boys are seen as unruly, guilty, and culpable for their actions. Then, when we grow up, Black women are deemed to be inherently hostile or angry, with a high tolerance for pain and without need for protection or care, and Black men are treated as criminal and thuggish — an ever-impending threat that necessitates putting down.

I mean, as a Black person, each one of us can easily and quickly recollect that first moment we were called a "nigger" and time seemed to split between before and after; you will never not know that feeling and knowledge of how others see you again. For me, it happened when I was in the sixth grade. A white boy named Peter, who I thought was a friend, simply stated it: "Get behind me, nigger." We were in line for lunch in the cafeteria, and I was completely caught off guard. I can remember it like it happened yesterday, not just the words, but also how it made me feel. I cannot imagine the quiet rage and heartbreak my mother must have felt when I came home and relayed the story to her that day.

Not long after that incident, there was an experience with my best friend, Pam, who was Jewish. She was having a huge birthday party but was like, "Well, you know... you can't come." Perplexed, I asked her, "What do you mean I can't come?" "Well, because you're Black." For some reason, she thought that the cause was apparent and self-explanatory. I am not sure if I hid the hurt in my eyes before putting my head down, but I did not consider her a close friend and sister from that day forward. To me, this was a betrayal.

So, somewhere around our pre-teens, it becomes clear to us that there is something different about us, a thing outside of our span of control, that we cannot change, yet will heavily impact the way we are not only perceived and received but also how we learn to show up. Because of prejudice and dehumanization from others, whether done consciously or not, we learn to respond in a way that keeps us, and those who look like us, safe and healthy. We are left to discover and employ coping mechanisms and strategies to endure and respond to myriad challenges requiring herculean strength to face the ever-present, day-to-day adversity of having deeply-melanated skin. Why? So that we can, at best, function in society, and at worst, live to see the next day.

EXISTENTIAL FEAR

This is why, for Black children, we begin to be stretched — even at a young age — because for our non-Black peers, the white kids, the world seems to be their oyster in some ways. They don't have to be so conscientious of not making a disturbance, not only with their presence but also with their voice. When a little white girl or a little white boy behaves like a child, they're seen as children doing all the things children do. However, when a little Black girl or boy does it, they are seen as disrespectful, animalistic, or acting out.

The majority group, Whites, do not see our children as innocent, and their level of empathy is diminished with time. Our babies, toddlers, and preschoolers are considered cute, but once they start to get some size to them, especially our nine-year-old, our thirteen-year-old, our sixteen-year-old Black boys and girls, they don't want to deal with them at all. I read a study that says Black boys are viewed as threats by their teachers beginning at five years old. What does that say about the education they will receive?

WHITE PRIVILEGE AND THE BULLY PULPIT

I grew up in what used to be a mostly white neighborhood. My sisters and I walked and biked everywhere, enjoying the freedom of childhood. At the age of about ten years old, however, that youthful liberty was stripped away and revealed to be a façade. One day, while walking on the corner of the neighborhood golf course to avoid walking directly on the street, a huge white man stopped his golf cart, came right up to me and shouted in my face that I had better get my Black ass off the grass. His anger, sweaty bovine body, and thick pointing finger in my face terrified the little girl that was me, which was precisely the outcome he had hoped to achieve. He wanted to terrorize me so that I would learn my place and not ever think that I was free to live and enjoy absolute freedom.

As I learned that day, racism is as much about enforcing a bully mentality as it is about protecting white privilege.

Whether it is over-policing our neighborhoods, penalizing our children too harshly, being followed while in stores, denied loans — and the list goes on — it is intended to forcefully deny our equal enjoyment of life. Eventually, for the Black child, the freedom of existence, expression, and voice is carefully and methodically erased.

As a child, this ingrained truth influences how we engage or interact as an adult. For instance, if I do not understand something, I may not raise my hand to ask a question since they might say I am disrupting the class, or worse, I am simply ignored. This response led me to become quite shy growing up; I walked with my head down and didn't ever want to read aloud in the classroom — and my mother is a former English and African American studies professor! She was like, "What is going on? Why are you so shy in school?" My teachers would say, "You went through the whole day without talking."

My reply? "Mm-hmm," because I was terrified of making a mistake and possibly causing an issue. I can remember someone telling me once, "Chauncia, it's good to be assertive, but make sure you're not seen as aggressive. I don't want anyone to think that you're aggressive." The reality is that it didn't matter what I did or did not do . . . my very presence disturbed them. Just showing up made me appear aggressive.

I had a sister-friend tell me that her response was exactly the opposite; rather than getting quiet, she talked all the time in an effort to be heard — to be seen. Not for attention, but to not become invisible, because she knew that she had something important to contribute. Nevertheless, she was seen as a problem and a source of irritation that needed to be tolerated or corrected. She said that if she wasn't being referred to the counselor's office for counseling, she was continuously being sent to the principal's office for discipline.

One time, when she was in a seventh-grade science class, she recalls responding to the teacher's question with what she felt was a simple answer. The teacher, a white man, paused as if he had been stung and then retorted, "Stop being so smart-mouthed! Why do you have such an attitude? Why are you being flippant?"

When trying to explain that she didn't have an attitude, that she was just trying to answer his question, she watched in horror as his face reddened as he became angrier and angrier with her. She wasn't cussing at him. She wasn't yelling. She wasn't calling him names or throwing a tantrum. She was just talking to him, yet he was utterly affronted by her.

This same scenario replayed itself in her adulthood. While working for a Fortune 500 Top 20 company as a Program Manager over a multimillion-dollar I.T. sales project, she remembers getting to the offsite "war room" earlier than the planned start time, grabbing a cup of coffee, and sitting at the conference table to read a book she had brought with her. After about fifteen minutes, the Project Lead entered the room and began booting up his laptop. Turning her chair toward him, she greeted him, "Good Morning." He said, "Good morning." And then, she turned back to her book.

Within seconds, he asked if she had prepared the assignment needed for that morning. She looked up, replied in the affirmative, and went back to reading. She will never forget what happened immediately following. . . he repeated what he had asked her, and when she again stated, "Yes," he flew into a rage — throwing his glasses onto the conference table, face reddening, spittle flying from his mouth, and yelling, "I asked you a question!"

You can imagine the shock she was in. It was seventh-grade science class all over again. How do you deal with that? What do you do? What do you say?

Throughout the remainder of the project meeting, she was ostracized, rejected by the other white members of the team because he was able to tell them about how this "aggressive" Black woman wasn't a "team player" and how terse and uncooperative she had been to him. Nobody asked her about her side of the story because, truthfully, her side of the story was told before she was born. Often, the stereotypes and biases at play speak louder than our voices, and no logical defense is welcomed or received.

· ·

*"If you're treated a certain way, you become
a certain kind of person. If certain things are
described to you as being real, they're real for you
whether they're real or not."*

-James Baldwin

· ·

Even to this day, I can remember a dentist I went to as a child; I was only eight or nine at the time, but when I told him that he was hurting me, his face contorted, he threw his instrument down and yelled so loudly at me, that my mother heard him out in the lobby. If she hadn't been there, I know that it would have been a much worse time for me. I was just a little girl, yet I still had that feeling that he didn't really want me there. And now, as an adult, I realize that he did not want to do dentistry work on that little Black girl. In my inexperienced youth, I sensed his frustrated anger and disgust. As an adult, I now fully comprehend the fright and intimidation he purposely left in my spirit.

There is so much stereotypical baggage that we deal with, which is a hidden pain that many Black people have. Our mistakes, our questions, our creativity, our voice is magnified negatively. And that's a burden we internalize, which can cause us to show up small or invisible in the world, or big and in your face to be seen and heard. You learn to shut down and say, "I'm just going to be quiet, do my work, get my check, and go on about my business," or you fight with everything in you to breathe.

And so, there comes the point when you have to say to yourself, "I must come out of my shell because I'm being suffocated in here. It is too tight in here, and I have something to say." And I genuinely believe that God has designed each person with what we need to accomplish the life-purpose He breathed into us when we were born (Gen. 2:7). Therefore, we have within us precisely what we need to perform and express who we were created to be. It's always going to want to come out of you.

However, when all these social constructs oppose you, or when the world's negative influences have been indoctrinated into your behavior throughout childhood and adulthood, it is imperative that you take a deep breath, process what is happening, regain your perspective, and *stretch* beyond it.

***

A REFLECTION: Part one has focused primarily on how our upbringing can color our perspectives of how society works. Now, I ask you to reflect on your childhood: What were some of the cultural aspects that framed your worldview? How has this impacted the way you view your place in the world?

Do you remember when you first realized that you were a minority or that you were seen differently?

_____

_____

_____

_____

_____

_____

_____

_____

_____

_____

_____

_____

_____

_____

_____

_____

_____

_____

_____

_____

_____

_____

_____

_____

_____

What are some of the coping mechanisms you have embraced and employed? If they have worked for you, share how. And if not, why not?

_____

_____

_____

_____

_____

_____

_____

_____

_____

_____

_____

_____

_____

_____

_____

_____

_____

_____

_____

_____

_____

_____

_____

_____

_____

PART TWO:
MITIGATION
Strategic Investments and Self-Assessment

> "If you can't fly then run, if you can't run then walk,
> if you can't walk then crawl, but whatever you do
> you have to keep moving forward."
> -Dr. Martin Luther King, Jr.

❝ *Chauncia, the City will* no longer need your services,"
the personnel chief said with a smile as he handed
me a termination memo. "Is this because I have filed a
discrimination complaint against this department," I asked?
He smiled again and said, "We don't have to give you any
reason to let you go. Now let's go to your office, gather your
things, and the police officer will escort you to your vehicle."

LIFE INTERRUPTED

And that was that. It was six weeks after I had made my
discrimination complaint to Human Resources, four weeks
after I met with the first attorney who told me to resign or

accept termination rather than fight, and approximately fourteen years after I started working for a local government that embodied structural racism in its every fiber.

No one ever wants to hear those words — you're fired — especially on a bright September morning — my son's birthday, no less. But when I heard those words, something inside of me breathed a sigh of relief that it was finally over. The years of torment and constant conflict at the hands of my employer were coming to an end. Unlike many women of color who have to endure discrimination, bias, and outright racist behavior on a daily basis, I was finally free.

I have been an Emergency Manager for many years, so I tend to look at life in the stages of disaster: preparedness, response, mitigation, recovery, and ultimately, resilience. When a disaster strikes, I immediately consider the current level of preparedness to reduce the disaster's impact on the individual or family, leading to a shorter recovery time.

So, when I was fired from that job, I had a myriad of thoughts run through my head: How was I going to feed and provide for my son, how was I going to pay the mortgage, what would I tell my parents who loved my "good government job," and would I have to live down the stigma? One of the first thoughts I had was, 'how did life prepare you for this moment?'

In reality, once I received those papers in my hands, I decided to hold my head up and walk out with dignity. I heard a still small voice whisper to me, saying it was time to go, no regrets; a feeling of strength and empowerment took hold of me and settled in my bones. I said to myself, 'you have the potential to overtake the world, and your passions and potential were never going to be recognized — nor your diversity appreciated — in this toxic environment where jealousy and deceit rule the day.'

At that moment, I acknowledged that my life's all too intimate experiences with gender bias, racism, stereotypes, etc., were meant for something greater.

But what was it?

> *"You don't make progress by standing*
> *on the sidelines, whimpering and complaining.*
> *You make progress by implementing ideas."*
> -Shirley Chisholm

MITIGATING LIFE'S DISASTERS

Life does not play fair; every day we live is unpredictable, so we have to plan for the ups and downs. Effective mitigation means putting in work before or after a disaster occurs so that whatever happens, the negative impacts are significantly reduced, and chaos is lessened.

As a woman of color, when life throws curveballs — those big nasty ones that we don't see coming, the kind that hit us right in the gut or the wallet, for that matter — we must begin to look for ways to protect ourselves from ever having that experience again. Whatever happens, we have to be able to recover. We have to intentionally position ourselves so that we have the upper hand and feel empowered to respond appropriately and land advantageously.

Here's the deal . . . Black people have to plan for life's punches much sooner than most because we do not have a safety net or trust fund to rely on.

I am the youngest of three girls, born in the mid-70s. Growing up in Florida, time with our family in Mississippi was an enormous contrast from our home in St. Petersburg, yet essential in terms of how I perceive diversity, equity, and inclusion. The most memorable thing was that I was surrounded by Black people. In St. Pete, we grew up around various cultures; still, though we saw poverty like you wouldn't believe in Jackson and Meridian, we didn't have that familial closeness in St. Pete.

My parents divorced in the early 80s, when I was still relatively young, around six years old. Looking in from the outside, you would probably think we were doing okay. But when they divorced, my mom became the head of our household, and in those days, just as it is today, teachers didn't make a lot of money. So, with all three kids living with my mom, she had to work three jobs and often borrow from friends to pay our bills. Daddy always gave a portion of his check, but some days we made do without electricity; other days, we had no cable. Food was rarely plentiful, and our clothes were often secondhand.

I can't say we were the happiest kids in town, but we were the most respectful, hardworking, and studious. Before Dad left our home, he taught my sisters and me how to mow our lawn, trim the bushes, rake the leaves, and generally provide upkeep of the house. Every Saturday morning, before Soul Train came on the television, you could find us working outside in the hot Florida sunshine. In addition to taking care of our house, we also cleaned houses for elderly or sick neighbors with mobility issues.

My mother didn't shy away from exposing us to the realities of life. Cleaning the home of someone that was dying of cancer gives you an appreciation for the value of life and a certain kindness that comes from knowing everyone won't be with you always. In all, having two parents who were raised in utter poverty gives you a hunger to use time to your advantage. Mom also ensured that we were all avid readers, encouraging us to read a new book each week. Often, historical novels or slave narratives caught my attention and could transport me to a different time or place in an instant. Even now, reading a good book on a specific time frame or event in history is a favorite pastime of mine.

I learned so much about life and my identity as a Black woman from my mother and father. In America, Black fathers are often referred to as "Deadbeat Dads" and Black mothers as "Welfare Queens." Welfare was created for white women, and when Black women sought to use the same benefits, the political conservatives called it abusing the system and labeled them. These particular racial metaphors are now rooted in America's anti-poverty policies, which have become generally accepted descriptions that effectively diminish the negative impacts of racism and injustice on Black families. The narrative causes one to assume that Black women seek to take advantage of the government and that Black men, more than any other, have babies with multiple women and do not take care of them. This narrative is false, and though it has been internalized by many, including Black people, data shows that Black men are much more involved with their children than white men who are not in a relationship with the mother.

Though my parents were divorced, my dad was fully involved in our lives, and he always lived within walking distance — promising to never move to a location further than his girls could walk to get to him. Sometimes, I wonder what it was like for him, a Black man, raising children in a world that viewed Black women so harshly.

BLACK WOMEN IN AMERICA

Both of my grandmothers were cooks. At the time, their primary choices were in service-oriented industries: A cook, a housekeeper, a nurse, or a teacher. The work was hard and the hours long, and many, if not most, were subjected to systemic, overt racism while working in white households. This is the reason my mom decided to become a teacher.

Growing up as I had, I was well aware that Black women in American society were not protected or highly regarded on any visible platform. As a young girl, I watched my mother suffer the effects of discrimination at work on a college campus and how it eroded her self-confidence and professional dreams. White students who did not like their grades could go to the department's chair or university provost and complain about Momma with impunity, the result being that she was often forced to change their grades. It was baffling and at the same time enraging that these students who had not earned their higher grade felt entitled to it because a Black woman did not have the authority to grade them down.

On Friday nights, I made sure to sit within hearing range as she and her girlfriends shared long conversations about their battles at work that week over a glass of sweet, fruity wine. The dialogues often veered towards their experiences working in white spaces where they were not respected or valued.

Now, my mother is still jazzy, and back then, she and her friends were some of the most well-educated, articulate, and poised women you could ever meet. They were to me like shiny diamonds, so intelligent, quick-witted, and beautiful, they lit up the living room. But, as I listened to their stories, I knew that I would not ever want to endure their workplace experiences for myself.

I mean, it seemed like every week, there was a different attack, despite acumen and ability. So, while I admired my mother's tenacity, I was well aware that there would be an intentional effort to diminish accomplishments and "keep you in your place" in white spaces. Her only defense was her extensive education. After all, she couldn't say she was a family friend of the dean or related to the school's provost as white people could.

Those nepotistic relationships are not common in the Black community, and in fact, if relied on, will cause additional scrutiny and accusations. Most of America's decision-makers in positions of leadership are white males, still to this day.

Therefore, in a world that does not promote or positively depict Black women in any realm, a Black woman's education and self-confidence are the most vital assets to survival.

SYSTEMIC MARGINALIZATION

Our family used to own the land where Jackson State University stands; however, we lost it through racialized acquisition, which is important when you consider much of Black people's current financial inequities exist today because many businesses, including land and property, were burned down, charged higher taxes, fees, and interest, or simply taken — the successful Black man beaten or lynched.

During that period, the American government, the Ku Klux Klan, and other organizations systematically attacked the growth of healthy Black communities, as they did not want us to thrive and become self-sufficient. The intent was further marginalization, social and economic exclusion to keep Black people in an undesirable societal position. Many Americans either do not know or do not care to see the nation's history of marginalization and how that impacts the lack of generational wealth for Black families in America.

These days, Black women make up the fastest-growing segment of college-educated adults, although you would never know it by how the media portrays Black women. Education, however, is still a useful tool in mitigating the negative impact of life's disasters, and because of that, education is a big thing in my family.

While most Black families have first-generation people with degrees, in my family, we are second-generation degree holders. My grandfather, even though he was an alcoholic and probably hadn't finished high school, repeatedly said, "The one thing the white folks can't take from you is education." And when you think about his reality, when he saw land ruthlessly taken by white tax collectors for nefarious reasons, Black people's freedoms lost due to an unjust policing and justice system, businesses burned by angry white folk who didn't support Black business ownership, and so on, you can see why having something that can't be stolen away was so important for him. Therefore, it's a huge reality for me and has been used to mitigate income loss. Everybody in my family is well-educated. You didn't have a choice not to be! So, education is critical to mitigating the disasters of life, as is having the confidence to bet on yourself.

When I was seventeen, my mother suggested I move to France even though I didn't speak French. She said, "You say that you want to become a chef, well then go to the Cordon Bleu. I hear it is the very best!" But I was like, "Ma. I don't speak French." Her response? "You'll figure things out." So yeah, my mother has always been a champion of taking calculated risks and being independent, not content with the belief that what we see is the end of it. Failure was never an option. It still is not, which is very scary sometimes.

The independent outlook my mother instilled in me has served me well, as she intended. She knew that I would have to contend with professional rejection in the workplace based on uncontrollable variables like gender and race and that I could not let self-doubt or fear of failure make decisions for me. She understood that my diversity was a benefit and that I needed to be comfortable in uncomfortable spaces where my noticeable differences could hinder me if I allowed it.

THE PARADIGM SHIFT

I believe that nothing happens by accident, and all things are known before they physically manifest. My core belief is that absolutely nothing catches God by surprise. Yet, in saying that, I know some things happen in life that causes us to question how a God that loves us so deeply could allow certain traumatic events to occur.

Some things impact us so dramatically, they change the way we perceive everything in life after that.

As I write this book, the nation is being challenged by the Coronavirus pandemic, which has had more deadly consequences for Black, Indigenous, and People of Color (BIPOC) than whites. The pandemic response has exposed the harm caused by existing inequities, those inequities that are rooted in racism, which lead to poverty, lack of access to health care, and so many other disparities that saturate the lives of Black and Brown people. At the same time, the country is reeling from the televised murders of George Floyd, Ahmad Aubrey, Brianna Taylor, and so many more, and coming to the realization that police brutality against people of color is a reality and there is a pattern that demonstrates the biased policing.

For me, 2020 represents a shift in trajectory, a defining year of revelation and exposure. From white people finally acknowledging the impacts of structural racism, à la police brutality, disparities in BIPOC death rates from the Coronavirus, to seeing white privilege exercised by a corrupt president and weaponized by cantankerous white women now named "Karens." So many unjust systems and perspectives were revealed and exposed in one year.

But I still ask myself, why us? Why were marginalized people's sacrifice so profound and the pain of loss so pervasive in the most vulnerable communities pre-2020? I think the answer is that the world had to be paralyzed and rendered immobile so that people's suffering could no longer be ignored or unseen.

There's an old Jamaican saying I love that says "If you cannot hear, then you must feel." It's used for disobedient children, but it applies here very well. White America chose not to hear or see the suffering of its most vulnerable people, and now, it must feel the pain of disaster, disease, and chaos. From the pain, stretching and healing will be birthed. Catastrophic disaster creates paradigm shifts and redirects the trajectory of our personal perception, and paradigm shifts fundamentally alter our thinking and behavior.

The world is experiencing an intense paradigm shift on many levels and now, at the same time, has a mirror held up to it that reveals its lack of exceptional clothing. Once seen as dominant, exceptional, and progressive, in one year, America's dirty laundry has been exposed, and it stinks to high heaven all around the world. From civil unrest and a host of disasters, including unending hurricane seasons and wildfires, to economic depression and a government that has become destabilized by a corrupt administration — the list of foundational shifts goes on.

I'll use one of my favorite Black colloquialisms: America is "shook." People are experiencing upset as their perception of proper cultural order is being challenged and reordered in real-time.

The cognitive dissonance, or distress felt when two or more ways of thought contradict each other, is happening to many who believed in white American superiority. Donald Trump and his administration have demonstrated that the white male is given free rein to be astonishingly incompetent. We'll talk more about that later. Really, who would ever think that America would be exposed for what it is? An imperfect fantasy allowed to exist in ignorant bliss for centuries.

One thing is certain: Adversity produces opportunities for growth and change. 2020 signified an opportunity for growth to me. America's faults were hidden and glazed over for so long, and now, the mirror that is the year 2020 reflects a broken country in need of stretching for survival...

STAT!

***

A REFLECTION: This chapter touched on the catastrophic disasters that occur at some point in everyone's life and how to mitigate their long-term impacts. What disasters have you managed in your lifetime and how did you lessen the negative effects of trauma?

_____

_____

_____

_____

_____

_____

_____

_____

_____

_____

_____

_____

_____

_____

_____

_____

_____

_____

_____

_____

In what ways have you created a dependency on the traditional paths of employment that would keep you feeling professionally insecure or ill-prepared should an unplanned change occur? What can you do now to strengthen your independence?

_____

_____

_____

_____

_____

_____

_____

_____

_____

_____

_____

_____

_____

_____

_____

_____

_____

_____

_____

_____

_____

Have you experienced workplace attacks? How did you respond to the attack? What is your experience in supporting marginalized groups in their struggle for equity? As a member of a marginalized group, what do you need to feel supported and heard?

_____

_____

_____

_____

_____

_____

_____

_____

_____

_____

_____

_____

_____

_____

_____

_____

_____

_____

_____

_____

_____

_____

_____

_____

PART THREE: RESPONSE
The Value of Diversity, Equity, and Inclusion

> "Equality is giving everyone a shoe;
> Equity is giving everyone a shoe that fits."
> -N. Dosani

When we think of diversity, many of us conceive only of diversity in race and gender. We are quick to discuss the answer to the singular question, "How many Black and Brown people do I see at the table? Are there any women present?" And, if we consider ourselves truly 'woke,' we may even go one step further and follow up with a secondary question: "How many Black and Brown women do I see?"

But, if that is as far as we are willing to go toward comprehending the myriad complexities of what makes for a diverse environment, we will miss recognizing the necessary grassroots work effort required to provide for an increased cadre of individuals within a workspace primarily dominated by heterosexual white, male (or female) professionals.

Why? Because we need to get beyond the antiquated idea of merely filling a quota or only putting a person of color (POC) into a position to check the box of diversity isn't the proper response to the issue. Nor does this knee-jerk reaction resolve the need of the individual being slammed into the slot, which is why an expansive working definition for diversity moves beyond a Black and white discussion. Instead, it is a variety of all of the qualities that make people different. In other words, it is not only the inclusion of a minority group; it is so much more than that single perspective — true diversity envelops the myriad of differences that make up a group.

THE VALUE OF DIVERSITY

The truth is, even if a room is filled with people of color, it is quite possible that an organization will still lack diversity; therefore, diversity for me, is the wide range of human differences, including but not limited to race, ethnicity, sexual orientation, age, gender, political beliefs, gender identity, physical ability or attributes, religious or ethical values system, national origin, and social class. The diversity of an organization speaks to its intentional efforts that permit differences to coexist while allowing for everyone represented — along with the qualities that make them different — to be understood, appreciated, and embraced.

Having worked in the field of disaster management for over two decades, I can honestly say that I have never experienced what it is like to be a part of an organization that values diversity.

First of all, the field of emergency management is overwhelmingly white. According to the U.S. Census, over 82% of leaders in the field identify as white, and over 71% are male! Those numbers are astonishing when you contrast the data on the makeup of groups most negatively impacted by disasters. But why does a lack of representation even matter?

It matters because homogeneous groups cannot produce equity; diversity and equity are interconnected. When diversity is absent, so is equity, and that is a massive problem for a field that prides itself on helping people in need, before, during, and after a disaster.

And really, that's the key to understanding the value of diversity: The harmful impacts of its absence. As a child, my upbringing and many interactions with society's dominant group were indicative of America's legacy of colonialism and oppression. Those experiences prepared me for the life I would be called to lead.

UNDERSTANDING EQUITY

I often use this quote during speaking engagements because I feel it most adequately explains a very complex concept in an unsophisticated way. Equity is about understanding the needs of those you serve and applying their perspective in solution building. In times of disaster, diversity and equity become critical and must be operationalized. Groups that lack diversity in perspective will not develop equitable policies, perform equitable planning nor create equitable programs that will benefit, rather than harm, the most vulnerable groups and communities.

Those who have enjoyed privilege sometimes have difficulty understanding the value of equity. Many will hear about equity as a theoretical notion and get really excited about it, vowing to fight for it with passion. Privilege approaches equity with a very surface level perspective that misses the nuances and complexities that exist beneath. This is why I think it is impossible for non-diverse groups to produce equity in policy, plans, or programs because they live outside of lived experience or intimate exposure. Those groups, boards, volunteer organizations, etc., begin creating plans and programs that do not produce equity, which may actually generate additional harm. Diversity in perspective and experience matters and is a requirement for embedding equity.

When you have lived a life entrenched in inequity, like so many, the approach to producing and implementing equity tends to be much more meaningful and have more profound impacts. For example, when you have lived your life in a wheelchair or relied on mechanical mobility devices, the understanding of access to facilities and ease of entry is a priority. In contrast, for those who have not had your experience, it is an afterthought.

Therefore, when people create plans and policies, they must require representation from the community and consider the existing inequities of those community members before planning. Understanding existing inequities will provide a greater understanding of the diversity that is needed at the table.

CULTIVATING EQUITY

Have you ever seen a picture of all white males in a meeting discussing a difficult decision, new policy, or crisis response? Whether they are disaster volunteers, government officials, or corporate executives, I can guarantee that whatever plan or policy they crafted was based on their own mutual perspectives and will probably most benefit the people that can identify with them and their backgrounds. Further, some assumptions are made based on shared experiences, especially since they do not have variety in perspective to draw on. That image of exclusive privilege has played out for decades in workspaces across the country and the world.

Cultivating equity in any realm requires first understanding the existing inequities that are at play. Too often, organizations will determine the need for increased equity but fail to approach the solution armed with diversity of thought and representation, as well as a knowledge of societal imbalances that created the need for additional equity measures in the first place. It is like putting a fresh blanket over a pothole and convincing everyone that the new blanket will solve the core problem of failing infrastructure. Real-life does not and has never worked that way. The pothole exists, so address the problem with well-thought solutions.

America has a wealth disparity problem rooted in systemic racism, which contributes to a plethora of inequities exacerbated in times of disaster. Every major system and institution in this country is led by white people: U.S. Congress is 90% white, U.S. governors are 96% white, the ten wealthiest Americans are 100% white, people who decide which books we read are 90% white, people who determine what news is covered are 85% white, and the list goes on. The default setting is the Anglo-Saxon white male, and this country has been structured to support him and those protected by his position in society.

According to a Pew Research Study, Americans generally think being white is advantageous in society, while at the same time, about half or more say being Black or Hispanic hurts people's ability to get ahead. That tells me that most people know and acknowledge that our country is structurally biased against people of color and that skin color is a significant determinant of wealth status.

Groups that lack diversity are hindered in their ability to produce genuinely equitable solutions. As a woman of color operating at a senior level in emergency management, my perspective was centered around equity. It made sense to me to produce programs that would benefit those people and communities most in need of support. My desire to focus efforts on vulnerable groups was often at odds with the organization's leadership, especially when led by white men who had difficulty prioritizing people of color and other marginalized groups.

Throughout my career, I worked very hard to implement programs for low-income residents, the elderly, non-English speakers, etc. I have even created regional business councils to assist low-income residents and families with multiple children, yet as before, these initiatives always garnered a negative response from leadership. The appetite for operationalizing equity to benefit those most vulnerable in a disaster within an organization must be present for equity to take root and flourish. As a Black woman attempting to explain the value of creating impactful, equitable plans, programs, and policies, I found that my voice was systematically silenced — similar to a radio being switched off.

Unfortunately, the silencing of a woman's voice in male-dominated professions is not a new thing, particularly when our unique perspective is not valued or respected. Like me, many women have dealt with the humiliation of being diminished intentionally and publicly by our organization's leadership, management, or co-workers. We have been silenced through lack of promotion, demotion, termination, or professional exclusion. All too often, our presence and perspective are not accepted, and we are simply tolerated because we meet the requirements for a quota the organization has set.

"It is time for parents to teach young people early on that in diversity, there is beauty and there is strength."
-Maya Angelou

INCLUSION AND BELONGING

As you know, my name is Chauncia. I am almost sure you have never met anyone with my name, and when we meet one day, you will surely tell me that my name is beautiful. I laugh, but believe it or not, that was not always the case. In America, difficult to pronounce or ethnic-sounding names are not appreciated and often serve as a mark of separation from cultural standards of respectable names.

It took me a long time to appreciate the unique name that I was given at birth. I can remember as a child, dreading having someone read my name or having to say my name during introductions because I knew they would say, 'now how do you say that, is it ...?' I picked up on that overt desire of others to make me understand that my name was not acceptably common and was different.

Different meant I did not belong in this mainstream culture of America. I see it all too often, with other non-white Americans ostracized and penalized for having names that are not standard European fair. This pressure to choose a European sounding name so that at least your name fits the norm is one of the most racist microaggressions committed against people of color. I have seen it with Asians, Indians, Africans, and anyone not named Karen, Becky, or Todd.

God made space in America and around the world for each of us to express our cultural heritage. The fact that one group spent so much time and effort to put a system of oppression in place is astonishing when you think about it. My name represents my identity, so why would I let someone butcher it or diminish it in any way? Some have said, "But those names are too hard to pronounce, choose something simpler." Says who? And when you think about it, how much of the European culture, food, language, and names have

Black Americans and Indigenous People of Color (BIPOC) been forced to learn and pronounce?

Imagine walking into a room and people having a preconceived idea about who you are, what you believe, what you eat, and your level of intelligence. Imagine they think these things as soon as you appear, based solely on your name, your skin color, or the way you naturally wear your hair. That is unconscious bias. That is the bias that occurs when you think about specific people or see them. It affects the way decisions are made and the way you conceive empathy and sympathy in your behavior.

This implicit bias is based on stereotypes and the belief that you are right in your thinking or worldview, which supports the programs you develop, the policies that seem right to you, and how you interact with those who are unfamiliar to you.

Implicit bias impacts decisions made around who gets a loan, who is promoted, and who receives that bonus at the end of the year. It is integral in everything you think, say, and do. Unless you actively unlearn your biases, you will instinctively rely on them in multiple areas of life, particularly decision-making.

"Our 2020 survey showed over 10% of respondents (underrepresented writers) reported being fired for pushing back on stereotypical characters/storylines and over 68% of BIPOC writers reported discrimination."
-Think Tank for Inclusion and Equity

Now, in the previous chapter, I discussed mitigating the impact that an inability to strategically invest in our future generations' capacity to build wealth has had outside the workplace — to be able to thrive beyond the pink slip — by shoring up transferable skills and experience and creating a sense of community; in this chapter, I want to share some thoughts regarding how to survive within the workplace when you are the only one who looks like you, thinks like you, shows up like you — when there is no one else who represents your lived experience, and the biases or stereotypes have become so pervasive that you no longer have space to move... to grow... to thrive! So, let's take a moment and revisit our working definition for diversity:

> The ability for a variety of differences to coexist, while allowing for each individual represented — along with the qualities that make them different — to be understood, appreciated, and embraced.

Unfortunately, being in an environment that is primarily white and male presents particular challenges, mainly related to an inability and unwillingness, in some cases, to respect and appreciate the value of diversity. Unfortunately, this breeds a systemic void, an insular bubble, that tends to be present, whether it is readily acknowledged or not. Those who resemble the majority, or accepted thoughts, looks, or behaviors will represent the prevailing norms — the "in" group — and those who do not have limited or no access to opportunities, voice, benefits, or other considerations. They will operate in a void —outside the bubble — while those within this bubble won't have to contend with many of the hurdles, hindrances, and obstacles that their "outside" counterparts face and deal with on a daily basis.

Then, when you consider that only certain voices, concepts, or ideas are being shared within this bubble, another issue is birthed . . . that of an echo chamber, which the dictionary defines as "an environment in which a person encounters only beliefs or opinions that coincide with their own so that their existing views are reinforced, and alternative ideas are not considered." Therefore, the same people are heard, the same experiences celebrated, and the same channels for new thought pulled from again and again. There isn't much diversity there at all!

Equally as bad is that many non-melanated people are oblivious to the reality that these issues exist and look at their Black co-workers as if there is something wrong with them if a concern is raised. We all know that this is our way of life in whatever industry we are a member of, but how do we survive this diversity void? What strategies can we employ to navigate white privilege, resistance to our assimilation, and the systemic lack of inclusion?

Before I share my recommendations, I want to first talk about white privilege. Many discussions are going on about what it is and even its validity as a concept or a thing. In my opinion, white privilege is simply the opportunity to be at a greater level of liberty "to do" or "to be" without the intangible restraints that Black people have to be mindful of. They can present or show up however they want to without being exceptionally challenged, questioned, or put on the defensive, even if what they are saying is inappropriate or untrue. Many times, I've heard my white co-worker say something that made me wonder, *'If I said that...?'*

I can remember times when I have had to defend myself because my boss received a phone call from the mayor regarding my "attitude" and saying things like, "I understand Chauncia had an attitude and didn't smile enough. She is intimidating and needs to smile more." I didn't do the "happy Black woman" character well that day, I guess.

This has happened more than a few times in my career; I have been challenged and disrespected because I didn't have that white privilege that says, "You're valid, and what you say, counts." As a woman of color, I know that we walk the road of bias and have to navigate the potholes of discrimination every inch of the way. Black women face more discrimination and bias at work than many other groups. Whether it's a problem with our hair, the way we speak, or our so-called "angry tone," the black woman's misery is the bias that other people carry.

"I've had to work hard for everything I've gotten in my life," is the retort I've heard time and time again to the statements regarding white privilege. Therefore, as it appears that many Caucasians errantly believe privilege only relates to wealth, being born with a silver spoon in your mouth, or things being handed to you, I will change the word to "advantage." It's a white advantage. Non-POC are automatically given the benefit of the doubt when they walk into the room; they are not negatively prejudged or seen as guilty and needing to prove themselves innocent of fitting the stereotype and able to override the unconscious bias of those in the position to withhold favor, benefit, or consideration.

White advantage is sitting at the same table I am, but starting with 100% inclusion rather than the fire-encased hoops I have to jump through to assure the other members in the bubble that I'm even worthy of being in the same room, let alone at that table. That white presence in the same space is esteemed superior, while my acceptance within the group is immediately deemed inferior due to the color of my skin.

> "So, the coping persona has been this mode of survival for generations of oppressed people. What I also learned through those experiences is that within our authenticity lies our real power and that's even in those environments, which by design, demand our complete and total assimilation to the patriarchy. We've been practically invisible."
> *-from the movie,* ***"Antebellum"***

As a whole, black people must decolonize the way we think about ourselves, our history, and our future. Our history and cultures are incredible; they do not begin in America with colonization and slavery. History has been revised to give BIPOC groups and the world a false narrative of who we are as people, based solely on the white supremacists' perspectives of the murderous colonizers and pro-slavery founding fathers, who peddled in selling, buying, and abusing our family member's bodies to benefit from the free labor.

That mindset of entitled superiority is evident in every crevice of America. However, the truth is that false superiority is based solely on the enactment of horrific violence and destruction against people of color. The mantra of the nation has been to kill them, abuse them, and steal the cultural components that are enjoyable, but keep them silent through perpetual deprivation of freedom, education, economic access, family, and power, in any form, create biased history and blame them for not attaining the "American Dream". The longer I live, the more I realize that accolades easily come when you walk on water and do what many perceive as impossible to do in their own lives. However, the moment their perception of who you are begins to sink . . . so goes their acceptance.

The other day, I reflected on the NBA players and their decision to not play basketball, because of Jacob Blake's death, to entertain the public. Basketball players are revered in America for their talent, height, and skills that seem supernatural. Yet when they stood up as a group and refused to play because of racism and police brutality, I heard more vitriol and affronted racism directed toward them than I have ever heard before. It came from those who felt entitled to see a good show, in spite of the player's plight, which is to be a Black man with one foot in a bubble and the other foot in the realities of oppression.

Jared Kushner, once again remarking on matters regarding those who have a different lived experience than himself, surmised it all by saying the players are very fortunate to be chosen to play and travel while being given a good salary. Those statements are akin to saying that slaves should not dwell on daily oppression but should feel grateful and happy that they are given one meal each day, and every so often, given a Sunday off to attend church. "Shut up and work," is what slaves were told to do.

When slaves arrived in America, many had their tongues violently torn out so that they would not spread their language and history or engage in unrestricted communication with one another. Now, silence is again demanded as we hear the question of why "they don't just shut up and dribble..."

As history is told, people will say that Donald Trump was the reason the country was divided, but I don't believe that's true — the country was already divided and infected with racism in all areas of its body. All Trump did was rip the Band-Aid off a festering, puss-filled wound called the United States of America. His blatantly racist behavior and the continued defense by so many of his actions and words have demonstrated to me how many people believe and feel just like he does. Ripping the Band-Aid off just revealed who we have always been as a country and that the old wounds of racism are just as fresh as they were when Columbus arrived to colonize the land.

Structural racism in the workplace and gender bias are inconvenient truths that many white people willfully ignore or do not address in their everyday lives. After the murder of George Floyd, one of the most brilliant things I heard was the suggestion that white people take "eight minutes and forty-six seconds" each day to contemplate structural racism and its impact on the lives of people of color.

Asking for that small amount of time to dwell on something so vast and monumental in Black lives doesn't seem like it would take a tremendous effort, but I wonder how many took up the challenge to do so.

This is the summation of the whole issue: We are invisible as individuals and as a people, which is why there is such a vitriolic reaction whenever we don't remain "in our place." And we have attempted for more than a few hundred years to assimilate into the majority culture — to be seen. But the truth is that we will remain invisible until we confidently show up as who we truly are and stop asking for permission to be. . . well, us. Because our future does not rest on how or if others see us, it is wholly dependent upon how we view or see ourselves.

Again, my name is Chauncia. Period. Full stop. End of story. And I don't have to accept the role, the position, the story that makes others feel comfortable around me so that they can "unsee" me — my brown skin, my history, my life. Therefore, I have decided to no longer try to assimilate, to become someone I am not, just to fit in. It doesn't work. It won't work. And although any discomfort of not doing so is due to perceived lack of access to value thought necessary for a certain quality of life, I have learned to integrate, to bring all the goodness that is me to every interaction, every encounter, every speech, every meeting, every appointment, every conference room, and every table.

STRATEGIC RECOMMENDATIONS

This is my recommendation to survive the diversity void, and following are three strategies we can begin to employ when we have to navigate white advantage, resistance to our assimilation, and the systemic lack of inclusion:

1. **Build alliances to support you, your perspectives, and your vision:** No one has ever fought a war by themselves and won. Everyone needs support along the way to achieve their best and show up, each day, with a mindset that says, "I can win". Sometimes, especially when we experience what I call 'professional isolation', it can be hard to see the value of nurturing relationships with other people in different departments, organizations, and associations. However, it is critical to form partnerships with external groups that will support you and the talent you bring to the table.

   Jesus was never appreciated at home. I can remember being requested to speak at national conferences all over the country, but being excluded from meetings within my own department. Had I not had so much support and encouragement from the relationships outside of my office environment, I might have never known that I could be successful without that job.

   In addition, there were times when I had friends in other departments call me to let me know what was being said, or done, that would negatively impact me or my division. There were even times when other department heads would let me know that my own boss was speaking negatively about me and my desire to direct support to underserved communities.

It's like a ram in the bush . . . you have alliances that provide support and have your back, even when you don't realize you need it.

2. **Be strategic at playing your own game:** I have been told that I should learn to play the game — a white fire chief told me that once. I was at a grant meeting and wondered why he would want to waste money on another command vehicle and he said that if I scratched his back, he would scratch mine.

I have seen the game played and even attempted to play it for a while, but, at the end of the day, my face does not fit. I am not one of the guys and I will not ever be invited into the good ole boys club. All the strategies that I've ever read in leadership books say that I should learn to play the game within the organization. But that is not possible when your face does not fit. Also, why should I assimilate to become someone that is not showing up as a whole, authentic being?

Let's be real . . . there's nothing like feeling trapped when you don't have options and believe that the game you've been set into is the only game in town. It's not. But, if you are going to play their game, at least do it your way: Build alliances, get folks on your team, and build those relationships so that they can be in the room speaking for you.

3. **Build your own playground:** It is important to have options. Investing in education, certifications, and alliance building will provide options and exposure to potential opportunities. And, don't forget to monetize your passion and expertise; the best investment you will ever make is the one you make in yourself. It will be difficult, but do not quit. People may not see the vision, but it is about your belief system. To build your own playground, you must know the wonder that is you. Each of us was created with unique abilities that no one else has. Those abilities align perfectly with our purpose.

In the space of diversity and inclusion, we often say that everyone deserves a seat at the table. I, however, want to create the table. I'm no longer willing to wait until someone decides I'm worthy enough to sit at a table they have set. Because if they can invite me to it, they can also uninvite me.

"Belonging doesn't require us to change who we are; it requires us to BE who we are."
-Brené Brown

Here's the truth . . . America is in crisis, and it must yield to being stretched. Stretched beyond racism, stretched beyond bias against women, stretched beyond any of our differences. We must begin to accept one another and adapt to the paradigm shift that has surfaced.

The pandemic has one hand, and racial reckoning has the other, and America is being stretched between the two. If we are to survive as a country, we must allow and demand that room be made for everyone to coexist. Without the necessary stretching that must take place, the world is headed for destruction. It is already showing signs of self-destruction. Still, the race toward diversity, equity, inclusion, and belonging is complex. It is a marathon and not a sprint. It's time to stretch toward the goal.

"New beginnings are often disguised as painful endings."
-Lao Tzu

It was December when the administrator I reported to called me into his office. It was late in the day, and I was writing an after-action report for a recent storm. He said, "I don't know why, but the big boss wants to know who the father of your child is. Also, he wants an explanation of why you should keep your job." I can remember standing at his office doorway and feeling like a 2x4 had just hit me in the stomach. I am sure my face reflected disappointment rather than shock because I was used to "the big boss" and his tactics that always singled me out. I immediately thought to myself, 'this is wrong' and replied, "I'm tired of being bullied by him. Why should I do that?"

My administrator sat back in his chair and replied that he didn't know why his boss disliked me and that it was in my best interest to just write the letter. He said, "You know, Chauncia, when you walk into the room, you intimidate. You have such confidence, more education than my boss and his entire executive staff, and you know your stuff. But it is you that he has a problem with."

As a single mother, a new mother at that time, my main objective was to keep my job. Here it was, the holiday season when everyone was preparing for Christmas break, and I must now write a letter explaining who the father of my precious little prince was.

The "big boss," a white man, had made terrible comments and vengeful decisions throughout my entire pregnancy. I can recall coming to work one day and being told that I would need to be driven home to retrieve my personal vehicle because the mayor had decided that I, out of twelve executive staff members, did not need a take-home vehicle. Here I was, the Emergency Manager for an entire jurisdiction, on-call twenty-four hours a day, in charge of managing the emergency management program and emergency operations center, now without an emergency vehicle. However, he did determine that the building custodian and facility manager should keep their cars, along with every other person on staff.

This man was accustomed to tough talk and bullying, particularly people of color, and behind closed doors, he was one of the meanest people I had ever had the misfortune to work for. Having worked for three jurisdictional leaders in different locations prior to him, I knew he was a rare breed of terrible. So, while I stood in my administrator's office, I determined that I must never put myself in a position where a white male could single me out and decide to exact his racist wrath on me ever again. I knew that the intention was to destroy me and my child, and because of the false narratives that jurisdictional leader openly promoted about me, I would never be allowed to reach full actualization of my potential. I could never imagine that a giant so big would focus his power on destroying me. Afterall, what did he see in me that stirred in him an urge to dominate and destroy? He saw potential. And guess what? Giants do fall.

As with David and Goliath's story in the Bible, I decided to use my resources to create a new path for my life. If the little shepherd boy had never encountered the formidable giant that was Goliath, he would never have become a wealthy king and ruler of many. So, instead of running from the giant, I picked up my slingshot.

I spent the Christmas break that year doing a whole lot of praying and a whole lot of crying, asking God to take the burden of fear and uncertainty from me. I had just bought a new house and birthed a new baby. What on earth was I going to do? By the time I returned to work, unsure whether my letter to the mayor had been received well, I was determined to forge a new path. The stress that came from years of being mistreated by my employer had turned my hair grey, but inside, my inner spirit was stronger than ever. I decided that no matter what happened, I would come out better than I was before. I made a list of everything I wanted for my life and the life of my child and gave it to God, deciding that faith must be tested to grow and that everything happening was only a test.

I now know that I can never run from giants, no matter how big they are. I must run towards them with confidence because they are blocking my success. My skills, gifts, and talents will make room for me to defeat the enemy, whether the enemy is a person or situation, but I must trust and believe it is possible. It took hard work to release the feelings of being inferior, inadequate, and insufficient brought on by workplace mistreatment. But I have realized that in life, there are giants that only I can defeat. All of the trials and tribulations that I went through for years were just boot camp preparing me for battle. Overcoming smaller battles and microaggressions prepared me for the larger battles to come, those battles that come with greater opportunities for increase and growth.

Years before being bullied by the jurisdictional leader and his senior staff, I had decided to invest in one element of self-improvement each year. I took classes, in-person and online, and sat for a professional review panel to become a certified life coach. After that, I founded a coaching business, though I never found time to get it off the ground; however, I considered coaching a skill set that could lead to successful monetization. In addition, I invested in a bit of real estate after learning I could use my 401K to invest in rental properties and took classes to understand the process of property investment and property management.

Every time I invested in myself, I opened up another pathway that would mitigate job termination or illness impacts that could cause a loss in my financial stability. I encourage all women to have multiple streams of income, at least three to four. Take an assessment of yourself and decide what skills, talents, and gifts you have that could create opportunities to monetize. Build up the armor of protection so that you never leave yourself vulnerable to someone else's whim, whether it is a job or in marriage. Be strategic concerning every move of your life.

When I think about my mother, grandmothers, aunts, sisters, and girlfriends who have endured the pain of discrimination in life and at work, I become re-energized to continue the fight towards diversity, equity, and inclusion. As women of color, we embody the intersectionality of gender and race, which helps to ignite ingenuity and critical thinking that shapes our intellect. Subconsciously, we know that we are judged using a different standard, but we also know that we have an extraordinary capacity to achieve great things. Hence, I stan the term "Black girl magic".

"Don't follow the beaten path, go where there is no path and leave a trail."
-Ralph Waldo Emerson

Emerson's quote speaks to the mindset of a courageous survivor; never stop learning, growing, or adding to your skillset. There are many paths to success, whatever success means to you. The days of the company man who stays thirty years to retire with the gold watch are pretty much gone. And then, like me, you can receive your "pink slip" at any moment — without discussion, explanation, or forewarning.

The reality is that a job can let you go or fire you, and you can't stop that from happening; but just because you lost the job or position, you cannot lose your experience, all of the knowledge you possess, or the skills you have acquired. These belong to you. No one can take them from you.

Therefore, the first way to mitigate the impact of cycles of poverty and society's rejection of who you are as you walk this earth in Black skin is to educate yourself. Consider it to be a form of intellectual protesting so that when the weight of it all hits you, even though your knees may buckle for a moment, you have the resources necessary to straighten up . . . and move forward.

***

A REFLECTION: This chapter has focused primarily on the value of DEI, while expounding on the concepts of unconscious bias, white advantage, and assimilation. Do any of the three strategies recommended resonate with you? If so, which of the three, if any, will you begin to employ, and why? If not, is there an alternative that you would consider?

What has been your experience with ethnic devaluing? How have you been able to navigate implicit bias, pre-conceived ideas of who you are and what you are capable of, and stereotypical behavior toward you in the workplace?

_____

_____

_____

_____

_____

_____

_____

_____

_____

_____

_____

_____

_____

_____

_____

_____

_____

_____

_____

_____

_____

What parts of you have you kept hidden or under wraps so that you can fit into the majority group? How can you now begin to integrate into the current environment without minimizing your authenticity?

PART FOUR: RECOVERY
Raising the Value Quotient

"So, each time a person decides to wait for
'time to change things', he or she is actually waiting for
other people to change his or her fortunes."
-Innocent Mwatsikesimbe

The day I lost my job, I had been late for work because I honestly did not want to go in that day, and the truth is that there were many days before when I would drive up to the job, park the car, and have to sit there for a few minutes and pray before getting out and going into the office. The interesting part of all of this is that two days prior, I thought that I needed to begin taking care of myself and heal from all of the issues and trauma I had been experiencing. Therefore, I scheduled an appointment with a mental health counselor, a nice lady who turned out to be a Black woman. It was a Wednesday, and I had booked her on a Monday.

As I sat on her couch after leaving the office with my box of personal stuff on the day I was fired, she said, "It's nice to meet you, Chauncia. Can you tell me what's going on?" And I said, "Well, today I was fired." After a slight pause, I continued, "It's also my son's fourth birthday today, and I wanted to take him to Legoland, but I don't think I should, because that would be spending money I really don't have."

Her answer caught me by surprise. "I know you believe in God . . . that you're a believer. And I guarantee that you're always going to remember this day. But from now on, each September 19th, you're going to celebrate and be thankful to God that this day happened." Perplexed, I started to share with her how terrible this day was, and she said, "It's not terrible. God gave you your freedom papers. You're sitting here with me because of all the trauma you've been enduring over the last five or six years is over, and now you're free."

Her words immediately created a mindset shift for me. I began thinking about things differently and understood why God wanted me to set up this appointment in advance of this day — making it so that I would go directly to the mental health counselor immediately following my job termination.

During this session, I also informed her that I was supposed to fly to New York in two days to meet with Columbia University over the weekend to discuss issues of diversity for marginalized and underserved communities. However, I would have to cancel because how could I pay for a hotel in New York, knowing that I wasn't going to have income coming in? Her reply? "Is the ticket booked? Is everything already set up?" I was like, "Yeah." "Then go! Because God has already ordered your steps."

Two things happened on that same day: An entity I had depended upon for my livelihood and welfare discarded my skills, experience, and contributions, and a Black woman I had never met before helped me to remember that my life is not in their hands — I bring all of that goodness with me and can recover everything I need to move forward.

So, on that Friday, while sitting on the plane, I noticed that my seat number was the same as the runway number. I was in alignment with what God was doing, and I whispered a prayer of thanksgiving to Him for the confirmation, "Okay, you're telling me I'm supposed to be here." And, I heard Him say, "I meant for you to go, and what happened yesterday wasn't a surprise. Nothing catches me by surprise."

And you know what? If I had paid attention, I wouldn't have been caught by surprise either, because there were so many clues to prepare me for what was about to happen. In all my years, when have I ever gone to see a mental health counselor, and I scheduled one on that exact day? Then, to top it all off, she was a Black female Christian. Precisely who I would need at that exact moment. Only God!

Now, the Columbia University meeting that weekend went exceedingly well, as I met with several organizations. It was the first time other people in my field of emergency management and those looking for guidance were open to hearing what we had to offer. Their response was one of awe. "Why hadn't anyone else thought of this? This is brilliant." — which also confirmed that God had given me the idea and that He had me on the right track.

To add more icing to this cake, my partner took pictures of me as I was speaking. Then he said, "I want you to put these on

LinkedIn, so they will know that they haven't defeated you." Which I did... and to this day, if you take a look at my timeline, you will see images of me speaking to groups of people only a few days after I had been fired. There is one picture with so many views that I'm sure it blew their minds because when others set out to harm you, they expect you to be under the covers, in the dark, crying your eyes out.

This taught me that we, as a people, need to see our value and that we are worthy of the same level of energy that we give to everybody else, the same level of high quality, and give it to ourselves to better ourselves. It was time for me to move beyond the mindset and traumatic conditioning of being a twenty-first-century "cotton picker" with an enslaved mind to becoming an owner of my future without limitation.

Recovery can be short-term, or it can be long-term. It's up to you. You decide how long you want to go through this, because for me, I said, "I don't want to spend any more time crying. I have spent, over the years, too much time crying and waking up to go back into battle again." And your heart gets heavy. Your body suffers. Your mind gets to a point where it's not functioning as well as it should. And I'll be honest, over the entire first year, I may have cried three or four times, but it wasn't about being fired, which is crazy; it was about being uncertain of what God was doing and unsure of the next step. I have a son to feed. I have a house and a car to keep. I need to make sure...

And now, I've gotten to a place where I'm like, "Okay, it's a process. You have got to go through the process." You can't jump the steps of the ladder; your foot has to touch each one. You must take the time to step back and acknowledge where you are, assess the situation, and recognize the skills, resources, and relationships you have available to build equity so that you can have longevity and increased sustainability. And so, it's a process that leads to rebuilding, to recovery, and ultimately, being able to create a legacy.

> *"We all should know that diversity makes for a rich tapestry, and we must understand that all the threads of the tapestry are equal in value no matter what their color."*
> -Maya Angelou

Still, I would be remiss if I left anyone with the idea that my Mach speed transition into solo-preneurship and self-employment has been a cakewalk. It hasn't. However, having good, encouraging people around me to help rebuild my esteem and courage was essential to strengthening a psyche that had been torn down. And so, I would want that for other people as well.

When your life has been flipped, turned upside down, make sure you don't surround yourself with a village of people who will continue tearing you down — shift toward your community, those relationships that shore you up. There was a moment even when my business partner was like, "You have all these people. You have someone helping you with speeches. You have someone helping you with this..." and

I got it. It clicked. That's when I made the decision to do something different and invest in myself — to no longer wait for someone to give me access, fighting for equality, but to require equity so that I can build a legacy for myself, my son, and for so many others.

According to a blog published in August of 2020 by the Annie E. Casey Foundation, equity is defined as "The state, quality or ideal of being just, impartial and fair." They go on to say:

> The concept of equity is synonymous with fairness and justice. It is helpful to think of equity as not simply a desired state of affairs or a lofty value. To be achieved and sustained, equity needs to be thought of as a structural and systemic concept.

From this, we understand that simply telling a marginalized group of people to pull themselves up by the bootstraps is ineffective and only continually serves to uphold the inequitable systems that are already in place. Why? Because equity goes further than "separate but equal" and is about making sure that everyone has what they need to be successful — which may not look the same for each individual or group since each person doesn't start at the same place or need the same things.

This is the primary reason why the enemy to equity is the failure to acknowledge that inequities exist. We cannot merely take broken systems and overlay them with "equitable" policies and expect positive impacts. Band-Aids don't heal gaping wounds. It's time to put away the Band-Aids, fix the systems, and embed equity.

And so today, America must now decide if it will commit to stretching towards equity — only time will tell if the commitment is only performative or if there will be some radical adjustments made for a better tomorrow for all citizens of the United States. We need equity in all things, all systems, and all structures that have institutionalized inequity. But first, it has to deal with its embedded system of racialization.

While most of our attention toward racism tends to be focused on symptoms, such as an overt and obvious action of being called "nigger," the country cannot win its war with the concept of equality until it contends with the deeply embedded system of racial inequity due to racialization — which has at its root, the twins of racial privilege and racial oppression.

As discussed earlier, where racial privilege demonstrates those advantages and preferential treatment based on skin color, racial oppression describes those disadvantages or limitations imposed upon a group based on their skin color. The Encyclopedia of Race, Ethnicity, and Society defines racialization as:

> ...the processes by which a group of people is defined by their "race". Processes of racialization begin by attributing racial meaning to people's identity and, in particular, as they relate to social structures and institutional systems; such as housing, employment, and education.

In societies in which "White" people have economic, political, and social power, processes of racialization have emerged from the creation of a hierarchy in social structures and systems based on "race". The visible effects of processes of racialization are the racial inequalities embedded within social structures and systems.

In short, racialization is an arbitrary grouping of others based on skin color while assigning a "place" within the system that matches that grouping. Throughout the most recent times, it has become a tool to be implemented to justify the inhumane treatment of non-white people, while slowly but surely transforming itself into colonialism, slavery, and then Jim Crow — while indoctrinating the notion that those who are members of minority races are fundamentally lacking and deserving of their lesser treatment. In comparison, members of the dominant race are seen as inherently superior and worthy of their better treatment.

Beginning in 2016, the country's legacy of racialization and misogyny was unveiled for all to see with an inept president in office who openly expressed racist, xenophobic, and sexist views, a terrible Covid-19 response that primarily impacted marginalized groups due to existing inequities, and the murders of George Floyd, Breonna Taylor, and Rayshard Brooks, among so many others, that revealed systemic racism in the justice system. I believe America is experiencing a thorough pruning that has resulted in the loss of life, a disastrous economy, and increased hardship and poverty for millions.

Before the murder of George Floyd, most of the country was blind and deaf to the continuous outcry of Black people who said time and again that the system of policing in America was biased against people of color. The sentiment was displayed frequently with comments like, "If you just do what the police say, you won't get shot," or "If you don't look suspicious and dress like a 'thug', you won't be stopped."

The victims of police brutality were blamed for inciting the police to treat them with violence, and it wasn't until people were forced to stay at home due to Covid-19 and watch a man being murdered on national television that an outcry of diverse voices was heard. Suddenly, people's sensibilities were shaken, and they were forced to listen to the cries of injustice and racism. Now, those cries cannot be unheard, and the cloak of willful ignorance about America's law enforcement system came off dramatically, people took to the streets to demand change in the structure of policing, and large corporations made statements supporting the Black Lives Matter movement when before, they would not have dreamed of affiliating with it.

Then, in November of 2020, a divided country decided not to re-elect Donald Trump, Jr., clearly rejecting the ideologies, systems, and policies that were against its non-white citizens . . . instead, choosing to elect a new president, Joe Biden and its first female vice-president, Kamala Harris — a woman of Black and South Asian heritage. Although this should be a celebratory moment for the entire nation, the very fact that almost half of the population voted to retain and continue and increase the previous administration's playbook of inequitable policies and systems is disconcerting, to say the least. Almost as if they are afraid that if the playing field were actually level, if everyone's needs were indeed met, then they somehow would lose.

See, the issue at hand is that when you've been taught and conditioned to believe that life is a zero-sum game and that if you don't control how the pie is sliced, you won't get any, you will do everything possible to make sure that others get the least amount of it — not necessarily by giving them the lesser portion, but by ensuring that you have the power over more of it . . . the best of it. So, yes, the others have been given access to the pie, which is equality. However, they can only have the crust, or the burnt part, or the small sliver in the corner that isn't enough to feed their families or build with, which would be equitable.

To help understand this concept a bit, let's consider a simple example: Homeownership. When you purchase a home or other property like land and pay down on the mortgage, you begin to build equity — that portion of value between what is owed and what the home is worth. If you were of the minority race throughout much of the twentieth century, your ability to buy a home — where you wanted — was prohibited by the employment of discriminatory and racist practices of steering, redlining, and covenanting were instituted and employed, without fail. Those giant billboards heralding in a real estate boom with images of beautiful houses, happy families, and new subdivisions along long stretches of empty two-lane highways didn't include pictures of people who looked like my great-grandparents or even my grandparents.

We were always relegated to ground zero, still at only equal, never able to gain the equity needed to flow into our children, our families . . . to move forward, thrive, build, and create a generational impact. That's the difference. This causes generation after generation to remain in a battle, a cycle of struggle, and you have to consciously and intentionally get your mind out of that survival mode and begin to look at what happened as an opportunity and become future-focused. Use that as a tool to the next phase, the next step, the next season.

> *"A lot of people want to skip ahead to the finish line of racial harmony. Past all this unpleasantness to a place where all wounds are healed and the past is laid to rest."*
> -Ijeoma Oluo

I am in no way certain that America can be stretched to achieve a growth that will allow it to reconcile its past atrocities, current failures, and future challenges. America must correct the existing inequities that have harmed people of color and other vulnerable groups because if it relies on Black and Brown people to facilitate the process of stretching, it will have failed before initiation. Therefore, the intentional work is in making a decision to stretch America in a better, more equitable direction while, concurrently, Black communities move from a reactionary posture to a more proactive one.

FROM REACTIONARY TO PROACTIVE

There is an initiative that has become the buzz of the African American community's hotline and has also captured the attention of the syndicated news circuit and various social media platforms; it is the Freedom Georgia Initiative.

This real estate project immediately piqued my interest — not only because of the media hoopla surrounding the movement nor the mass following it has acquired but also because their mission aligns with many of the principles that undergird and support the core values that I embrace and employ. It is a perfect demonstration of what I am proposing as one solution to creating a generational impact. So, I allotted some time and attention to research it.

The Freedom Georgia Initiative was launched by Georgia-based realtor Ashley Scott and her friend, entrepreneur, and investor, Renee Walters, and according to them, it was established out of a sense of extreme urgency to create a thriving, safe-haven for Black families in the midst of the current catastrophic issues of racial trauma and injustices, the global pandemic, and the economic instabilities existing across the United States of America brought on by COVID-19.

Like many of us, these ladies recognized a critical need to address the present instability of our culture and procure a resolution that would positively impact both our present and future generations. Recognizing that the established system was designed to oppress us rather than progress us, their determination inspired them to say, "We will build it ourselves." Which, quite frankly, is what I believe stimulated the generations before us to build their own so that they could take care of their own. Once the vision was established, these ladies shared it with a select few, and together with nineteen Black families, purchased 96.71 acres in Toomsboro, located in rural Wilkinson County, Georgia.

I agree that this initiative has the potential to be the prototype/model by which we can go about establishing an innovative community that is self-sufficient, environmentally sustainable, and that offers cooperative economics among BIPOC communities. The Freedom Georgia Initiative, LLC is Black-owned, women-owned, family-owned, and veteran-managed; and seeks to support the same by providing contracts to well-qualified vendors.

I lovingly applaud this group and its vision because I believe this proposed plan can construct communities that will become the modern-day versions of Rosewood, Black Wallstreet, and other successful, Black-owned and operated communities that once existed and thrived amid the tyranny of their time until they were ultimately destroyed. The Freedom Georgia Initiative will become a place that is built, owned, and operated by us — a place that is governed and policed by us. A designated space upon this globe designed specifically for us that will prayerfully exemplify the motto of the FUBU label: *For Us By Us*

Our careers, lives, and way to the future are no longer straightforward, stable, or moving forward along a predictable path. So, for us to truly achieve the level of wholeness, peace, and accomplishment we desire in the workplace, irrespective of how we are being perceived, we have to be aligned with who we are, understand our values — what drives and motivates us — and implement a plan of action that supports that.

> *"Knowing is not enough. We must apply.*
> *Willing is not enough. We must do."*
> -Bruce Lee

Make it a point to no longer leave your "fate" in the hands of those who benefit from your efforts while not having to deal with the realities of who you are. We must cease waiting for things to be fair, continually fighting for equality, and make the shift from being reactive to implementing proactive strategies to increase equity for our families, our community, and ourselves. It is the key to stretching from a state of recovery to becoming more resilient.

Success has always been an intentional pursuit. It never occurs by accident and requires pain to birth it forth; it requires stretching for growth and survival — a continuous investment in yourself. On the other hand, a failure to stretch is ultimately a choice to hinder growth and die. So, lean in and allow yourself to be stretched.

***

A REFLECTION: This chapter has focused primarily on the concepts of recovery in order to move beyond simply surviving in a society that doesn't demonstrate value for the other. What has your family lost? Keep in mind, this may not necessarily be property or land; it could be language, culture, traditions, connections, legacy, or other intangibles. Begin to tell your story here:

_____

_____

_____

_____

_____

_____

_____

_____

_____

_____

_____

_____

_____

_____

_____

_____

_____

_____

_____

_____

From the various strategies shared within this book, which one(s) will you implement for the purpose of becoming proactive toward recovering that which has been lost — not only for yourself, but also for your family and for your community?

_____

_____

_____

_____

_____

_____

_____

_____

_____

_____

_____

_____

_____

_____

_____

_____

_____

_____

_____

_____

_____

_____

What do you still need to do so that you can move beyond merely *surviving* to *thriving* in environments that don't value who you are and what you bring to the table?

_____

_____

_____

_____

_____

_____

_____

_____

_____

_____

_____

_____

_____

_____

_____

_____

_____

_____

_____

_____

_____

_____

_____

_____

_____

_____

PART FIVE: RESILIENCE
Stretching Beyond and Growth

> "The best way to not feel hopeless is to get up and do something. Don't wait for good things to happen to you. If you go out and make some good things happen, you will fill the world with hope, you will fill yourself with hope."
> -Barak Obama

My mom used to say that the very dirt has the blood, tears, and sufferings of so many; the soil cries out from the injustice of it all. So, when I think of resilience, I think about my ancestors, who were of Indigenous and African descent and robbed of their land, freedom, and humanity because brutal colonizers used deception to build America. They endured the atrocities of colonization and slavery yet were able to produce a lineage that exists in the present day.

Our forefather's sacrifice was ultimate, and indeed when I learned our DNA was changed as a result of the trauma caused by slavery, I took pride in understanding that resilience was now embedded. After all, their resilience led to my existence, and their ability to endure ensured generations would live long after they walk on in death.

Nothing truly remarkable and rewarding has ever been achieved without overcoming emotional stress and sacrifice to rise to the next level. And, although a part of me acknowledges that this country has never truly valued the lives of Black or Brown people or taken a sincere interest in their well-being — whether it's a catastrophic hurricane or global pandemic, people of color receive the lowest prioritization of effort — I continue to believe in the concept of a more perfect union . . . a country where all of its citizens are included, respected, and valued.

It will take pain and sacrifice, but anything worth having is worth shedding a few tears over, be it birthing forth a child, making it to the finish line of a marathon, starting a new business, maintaining a relationship, or moving beyond the mere illusion of inclusion.

THE ART OF INCLUSION

Inclusion... let's pause here and talk about that for a minute. According to the dictionary, the first definition of inclusion is "the action or state of including or of being included within a group or structure." However, now I have to look up what it means to be included, and one of the things I learned as a child is that you don't define a word by using the word you're defining, as it creates confusion or circular thought. So, as simplistic as this definition is, it cannot adequately express the complexity of the concept of inclusion because there is an art to it. What I mean is, true inclusion is not achieved by someone simply being a part of a group or structure.

Why not? Because it lacks belonging, and without a true sense of belonging, you only have the illusion of inclusion. And, according to the Mayo Clinic, we cannot separate the importance of a sense of belonging from our physical and mental health:

> The sense of belonging is fundamental to the way humankind organizes itself. If it was unimportant, we would live solitary lives, only coming together for procreation then quickly kicking the children out of our lives as soon as they could walk. We would have no families, communities or organized government.
>
> We begin life with the most crucial of needs: Attachment to a caregiver. This is the beginning of our fundamental need for belonging. Studies have shown that children who have not achieved a healthy attachment in their young life have lower self-esteem, a more negative worldview, are mistrustful and can have a perception of rejection. Depression, anxiety and suicide are common mental health conditions associated with lacking a sense of belonging.
>
> These conditions can lead to social behaviors that interfere with an individual's ability to connect to others, creating a cycle of events which further weakens a sense of belonging.

What this says to me is that you can be a member of a family, church, sports team, firm, or any other type of group or organization, and yet not feel as though you belong — that your whole self has been fully and entirely accepted. Therefore, what is missing is not the acceptance of your part into the whole, but all that you are is embraced within the entity, group, or structure.

Let me see if I can make this a bit clearer because, as I noted earlier, there is an art to this. So, let's consider the second definition the dictionary gives us for inclusion:

> The practice or policy of providing equal access to opportunities and resources for people who might otherwise be excluded or marginalized; such as those who have physical or mental disabilities and members of other minority groups.

I have italicized a few keywords in this definition: practice, of providing, access. Now, my thoughts were made known about the difference between equal and equitable in the previous chapter, so I won't repeat that here; however, I want to focus on these specific words because this is where most companies start . . . and stop — "We provided you with access." "We hired you and gave you a job with our company." "We brought you into the room and let you have a seat at the table." This, in no way, creates a sense of belonging.

The Society for Human Resource Management (SHRM) defines inclusion this way:

The achievement of a work environment in which all individuals are treated fairly and respectfully, have equal access to opportunities and resources, and can contribute fully to the organization's success.

That sounds good . . . we're getting closer. With this definition, we understand that there is more to it merely providing access; it includes an aspect of behavior — of proper treatment. Still, there has to be a reason why many talented, skilled, and high-level contributing minority hires are not seen in influential positions or holding titles of authority within the management teams. It is because the company has a "practice of providing access" while not extending that access beyond numerical representation to incorporating authentic and empowered participation and a true sense of belonging. The marginalized person cannot bring their whole self into that space, or as in many cases, participate in both the tangible and intangible benefits awarded for their contribution to the organization.

See, when you value people, you don't merely pay lip service to their presence. You don't just have their name on the roster and make use of their contributions while ignoring and then discarding who they are. It means that you include them, their voice, their ideas, their culture, their lifestyle, and their background. They will be made to feel respected, that their contributions are rewarded, and that they "belong." This is true inclusion. This is true diversity.

> *"Diversity is being invited to the party;*
> *Inclusion is being asked to dance."*
> -Vern Myers

For centuries, the default setting in America has been Caucasian, heterosexual male. Therefore, the policies, perceptions, practices, etc., are set to "white male," with white females closely aligned because they generally support their place in society's patriarchal status. Don't believe me? Then, consider the reality that 55% of white females voted to re-elect Donald Trump in the 2020 elections... a slight increase from the 2016 elections. So, even after more than three years of misogynistic, "grab-'em-by-the-pussy" speak, white women have agreed via their votes to continue to accept second-class status as it relates to their being female, as long as they are above others in race; including their Black and Brown sisters.

This is why I don't believe people when they say, "Oh yeah, we're diverse. We just hired a bunch of women," and the demographics of the women are Caucasian, with maybe one or two minorities. This is what I call "Band-Aid diversity". Their perspective is generally the same as the default setting, and they will do whatever they need to do to uphold their position within the "pecking order" or system.

The result of this is that while the dominant race may have a policy of inclusion within organizations and groups, the reality is that behavior will be driven by the need to protect the status quo, so although we are let in the door, we are never truly accepted... only tolerated.

THE PRUNING SEASON

This is the state I finally arrived at in my traditional employment. I was included, but there was no sense of belonging. I was always made to feel like an outsider — someone who had been invited to the party but never asked to dance. Therefore, I had to shift and do something different.

There is an adage that states, "Two minds are better than one," and in my favorite book, the Bible, it says that "two are better than one" (Ecclesiastes 4:9-12), which means that in many endeavors, it is beneficial to have a partner who can take the journey with you and offer a listening ear for ideas and decisions.

Like many women, as a single mother, I didn't have a sounding board in the form of a husband who could consider challenges and opportunities with me. Then one day, I was speaking at a conference and ran into my friend, Curtis, while there. He heard me present to an audience of emergency management leaders from across the nation concerning the topic of harmful impacts caused by a lack of diversity and inclusion in disaster management. I talked about victim shaming, anti-poverty biases, and the realities of racism in emergency operations.

After I spoke, he suggested we meet at the bar for a quick discussion about how we could change the outcome for vulnerable groups in disasters. Two hours later, the framework for the Institute for Diversity and Inclusion in Emergency Management (I-DIEM) came to life on the back of a napkin, and I now had a partner to build with who was completely onboard co-founding with the endeavor as a partner.

I have never believed that anything happens by accident or without reason. In much the same way, I view the year 2020 as a pruning season for America. The theory of exceptionalism in America was exposed to be a bald-faced lie. America is not exceptional, and though most of the country's history has been written to demonstrate victory and overcoming, the reality is that it is a country's people that make it exceptional. When people stand up for change and speak out against wrongs, the country can abound in exceptionalism and become all that it has proclaimed itself to be.

Nevertheless, in order to grow, to become more resilient, flowers must be pruned of anything that is dead or that stifles life. When pruned, some flowers will die while others will stretch towards the sunlight and flourish. With water and sunlight, those flowers will grow and provide their beauty to the garden where they are planted.

Life provides each of us with the circumstances and situations that prune us, individually and collectively as a country. Whether it's the loss of a job, divorce, financial hardships, whatever it is, life has a way of tearing away parts of our sense of stability and certainty. Those things that we were certain would happen or were comfortable with having are stripped away. I have learned that when our inner consciousness gets uncomfortable or restless, pruning is occurring. Pruning can happen in a big way with considerable reckoning or loss, or it can be a nagging discomfort that won't go away. Either way, a decision must be made on how to respond to it.

Pruning is not always a quick process and can take years. I can remember how uncomfortable I was at my job for three years before I was terminated — feeling absolutely out of place within the organization — but because I needed to work, I stayed. There were days when I walked into a meeting, and people would stop talking; or, I would submit paperwork and get denied conference attendance, even when the conference was in the same city! Life was pruning me and using that job to accomplish the mission. At one point, I can remember saying a prayer to God in recognition that a spiritual battle was taking place. Racism, gender bias, and all forms of bigotry are sin, and the spirit recognizes sin. I could also perceive change and transition but didn't know in what forms. All I could do was pray and document the process.

Stretching is a conscious decision that each person must make at some point in life, and during the pruning season, a time will come when a decision must be made. It will be the decision that determines your next phase of life . . . whether or not to stretch toward the sunlight. It is the choice to succeed despite failure, unexpected change, or loss, essentially to lean into being stretched. As I experienced the pruning process at work, I spent more and more time thinking about the future and visualizing what I wanted my life to be. I discovered that as I envisioned a different life for myself that was not dependent upon working in that job, new opportunities to use my gifts and abilities presented themselves in unique ways.

The pruning of America began years ago and continues to this day. However, marginalized groups cannot repair the damage because we are not a part of the dominant group that benefits from the current construct. In other words, those white people who support institutionalized bias must intentionally work to deconstruct the system.

> *"Inclusion is not a matter of political correctness. It is the key to growth."*
> -Jesse Jackson

THE SAVVY DIMENSION

Now, in my current role as co-founder and CEO for the Institute for I-DIEM, I have been given many opportunities to speak around the country and host mastermind groups for women and people of color in leadership. For many, the mindset of stretching can be difficult because it requires self-reflection. Also, stretching is a commitment that impacts all parts of your life. However, if we do not change our attitude about our circumstances and situations, we will miss our altitude!

I believe that if a person has breath, then they can be stretched, and once they have been stretched, they enter into another dimension of life. I call this the Savvy Dimension. This dimension allows us to achieve a successful outcome that was elusive prior to pruning. I think of it as the place where the light switch has been flipped on, and there is a renewed hope for a successful outcome. It is the time and space when hope has replaced the pain in your heart, and your stretching transition has hit its stride. You know things are getting better, even as fears still exist. However, this time, you are savvy and have the expectation of harvest, of growth — you have experienced utter disappointment and decided to overcome. Through pain, uncertainty, and loss, you have learned the lesson of what it takes to be successful and to sustain success.

Entering the savvy dimension could not have occurred before stretching because we would not have acquired the needed knowledge and experience to recognize uncommon opportunities and manage the benefits achieved. Still, while this dimension comes with new opportunities and responsibilities, unfortunately, pain and discomfort pave the way to the savvy dimension. Nevertheless, many people will say that they wouldn't trade the pain and heartache experienced for anything because it taught them so much. I feel that way about experiencing divorce and losing my job.

See, going through my divorce was one of the most painful experiences that I have gone through. The pain I felt from being in a marriage with an adulterous man was nothing compared to the pain of actually divorcing that unfaithful man. Knowing that I would have to tell my family and the world that I was making the impossible decision to go in a different direction in my life felt unbelievably painful. Day after day, waking up with the recognition that the life we planned together was not going to happen and that our twelve-year love story was coming to an end was pure devastation — but not defeat.

Similarly, losing my job and realizing that life was unstable and uncertain was also devastating but not defeating. Acknowledging the stigma, the impotent anger, the feeling of anxiety so pervasive I couldn't sleep at night helped me tremendously. In every situation, I allowed myself time to mourn the loss and slowly but surely, begin to look for the sunshine.

That's what we have to do to stretch . . . because sometimes, life drops a boulder right on top of your world, and then, once you realize that you're still breathing, you figure out a way to crawl out and push that boulder downhill. That's when I know that there is a blessing in the pain, and I need to take what I have learned from the experience to make the next phase of life better.

So, I can genuinely say that you must allow yourself to be healed from the negative results of your past defeats; if you are going to walk amongst people with affluence and influence, you cannot have a countenance that does not reflect the renewed hope of success and life. As we move towards a better future, we must commit to stop looking in the rearview mirror at our past. Focus on the future and what is in front of you. Think about a car and how much it would be impossible to drive it if you are always looking back at what you've already passed by and the mistakes that you made. Look towards where you are going and have a map with you so that you can identify the direction that you would like to go.

And, as a country, can we win the race towards diversity, equity, and inclusion? Of course, we can! However, to do so requires leaning into being stretched . . . and to be stretched is to become resilient. So, we must choose to stretch towards a society that respects diversity, prioritizes equity, and welcomes inclusion in all structures and systems. The journey will surely evoke tears and heartache over the years, but the struggle is well worth the outcome.

***

A REFLECTION: This chapter has focused primarily on the concept of resilience and how to begin stretching and growing. How do you define resilience and how has this been demonstrated in your life?

_____

_____

_____

_____

_____

_____

_____

_____

_____

_____

In what areas have you felt a sense of belonging? How can you recreate that reality in other areas where inclusion is not fully practiced?

_____

_____

_____

_____

_____

_____

_____

_____

_____

_____

_____

_____

_____

_____

_____

_____

_____

_____

_____

_____

_____

_____

As much as we try to avoid it, personal loss is a natural part of the cycle of life. So, reflect on a situation or circumstance that you have experienced and consider how you can use it to create something even greater that will propel you into the savvy dimension?

_____

_____

_____

_____

_____

_____

_____

_____

_____

_____

_____

_____

_____

_____

_____

_____

_____

_____

_____

_____

_____

A Challenge for a Better Tomorrow

> "When life gives you lemons, make orange juice
> and leave the world wondering how you did it."
> -Mitch Griego

N ow, you may ask yourself, how can one take lemons and make orange juice . . . wouldn't it make more sense to expect lemonade? But if you consider our cultural story, you may find that much of our experiences as a people, as a culture, actually supports the statement quoted above much better.

Our non-melanated brothers and sisters can boast of the sweet, heavily pulped orange juice they were able to make from the oranges they have been given, but as Blacks in white-dominated spaces, we have consistently been given less, yet achieved more. In fact, not only have we used less to accomplish more than was expected, even when it was not acknowledged or adequately appreciated by those who attempted to set us up for failure, we have consistently taken the scraps, the hand-me-downs, the broom closet, or the basement, and created and sustained a completely different outcome, invention, or lifestyle that is unique to us! In essence, we have taken the scarce or bruised lemons and made our orange juice, leaving others wondering how we were able to do it. Because we are now — and always have been — resourceful.

How do you think that we have been able to strive and survive amid a global pandemic even with minimal, suboptimal healthcare, with pre-existing medical conditions that cause many of us to fall into the high-risk categories, sadly causing our death rate to be disproportionately higher than the average? How are we able to unite and protest the ongoing racial injustices and blatant murders and abuse by those sworn to protect us? How are we able to survive when we are being ostracized and maligned by political powers in this nation's highest office, which is being openly supported by those who share the misguided and bigoted beliefs?

I will tell you how. . . because we have become proficient in thriving in survival mode. We have learned how to make orange juice out of lemons. So, my final thoughts come in the form of a challenge to each of you who have read and identified with my words and recorded your account of this subject matter.

Listen, America may never decide to take up the baton in the race towards diversity, equity, and inclusion. They may conclude that the process of stretching is too difficult — be it individually or collectively. The country is divided in a way only seen during the Civil War when the north battled the south, good versus evil. People will want to find a figurative Band-Aid to put over the wound that is oozing infection. Nevertheless, to survive as a nation, America must stretch beyond its past towards a more diverse, equitable, and inclusive future. This time, however, there can be no compromise; it must be all or none, no back room deals.

> *"Diversity is being invited to the dance.*
> *Inclusion is being asked to dance. Equity is*
> *allowing you to choose the music."*
> -Cynthia Olmedo

And, I know that it takes courage to speak up when you are being discriminated against — for whatever reason. The repercussions and retribution that women and men of color face is real and frightening. Speaking up or attempting to operate outside the diversity void can set an entire system against you to take your career, your good name, and steal your future. That's what they tried to do to me. But God...

Still, understand that nothing changes if nothing changes. It is not enough to acknowledge that these degrading issues exist or that we face challenges on an almost daily basis; we must be willing to equip ourselves with the tools and apply the principles that will transform each of us into change agents to promote a new reality. Therefore, I encourage you to dedicate some time to review the answers you've recorded and devise and activate your plan of action. Educate and engage others in this process and brainstorm together . . . make it a community project.

Let us take our individual stories and propose a process to initiate change; then let us use the wisdom we have acquired through our collective experiences and create a lasting and evolving change – One person. One story. One experience at a time. Let's begin the process of stretching toward diversity, equity, and inclusion... *together.*

About the Author

I grew up in St. Petersburg, Florida, in a close family of voracious book readers. My mom, an English Rhetoric and African-American Studies college professor encouraged us to read daily and acquire knowledge from books. From a young age, I was exposed to the realities of life, which influenced my perspectives on race, gender, poverty, and so much more.

I am a Certified Professional Coach, Cultural Diversity expert, and Emergency Manager. My expertise includes disaster management, national security event planning, leadership coaching, immigrant and refugee outreach, as well as diversity, equity, and inclusion training. In my role as CEO for the Institute for Diversity and Inclusion in Emergency Management, I am entrusted to lead the effort to integrate equity into all facets of disaster policy, programs, and practice with the goal of increasing cultural competence and mitigating the harmful impacts of bias on underserved groups.

I have gone through more skirmishes, battles, and wars in my twenty-year career than I care to remember. My experiences have taught me to prioritize my faith in God, trust my inner voice, and have confidence in my inherent talents and abilities. I have learned the techniques and mindset that are needed to grow like a rose in the desert.

I believe that anything living must be pruned to flourish. Life has a way of pruning us, individually and collectively, through pain and loss. We can choose to die on the vine or stretch towards the sunlight to grow beyond what we think are insurmountable limitations. Personally, I have chosen to be stretched...

For more information, visit:
www.chauncia.com

CPSIA information can be obtained
at www.ICGtesting.com
Printed in the USA
BVHW090321230221
600781BV00006B/992

9 781736 159316